Organize Your Office
and Manage Your Time

*Take steps everyday
that move you towards
your dreams!*

      Much Success,
      Tracey Turner
    Shawn Hansen

Organize Your Office
and Manage Your Time

A Be Smart Girls™ Guide

Dhawn Hansen, CPO®
Tracey Turner, CPO®

iUniverse, Inc.
New York Lincoln Shanghai

Organize Your Office and Manage Your Time
A Be Smart Girls™ Guide

iUniverse books may be ordered through booksellers or by
contacting:

iUniverse
2021 Pine Lake Road, Suite 100
Lincoln, NE 68512
www.iuniverse.com
1-800-Authors (1-800-288-4677)

Illustrations: Martha Geisler
Photos: Mayer Studios Inc.

ISBN: 978-0-595-42488-7 (pbk)
ISBN: 978-0-595-86821-6 (ebk)

Printed in the United States of America

To our clients, who encouraged us to write this book so others may benefit from our time management techniques and achieve the life they have always dreamed of.

Index

Acknowledgments

We would like to thank everyone involved in the process of creating *Organize Your Office and Manage Your Time*, the first in a series of Be Smart Girls Guides. Also to our clients, whose positive feedback regarding their successes with our programs encouraged us to write this book.

Many thanks to our talented illustrator, Martha Geisler, who made our visions a reality. Mayer Studios deserves recognition for our professional photo images. Thank you, Seth and Paula.

To our husbands, friends, and families, whose love, support, and encouragement made this book possible.

We are especially thankful to the universe for bringing us together—two girls from opposite ends of the United States meeting in California and creating a personal and business relationship that has been rewarding on so many levels. We not only have dispelled the myth that "women can't work together," but have proved that when we work together there is no limit to what we can do.

Mission Statement

Be Smart Girls™ is about getting more out of your life through organization, time management, and putting the SELF first in order to give the most to our families, careers, and friends. It is not about being selfish. It is about taking care of the hub so the wheel can turn without squeaking. It is not about perfection. (It does not exist). It is not about being a superwoman. That is what has driven so many of us to exhaustion and discontent. It is about making a plan. Be Smart Girls uses goal setting and time management tools to help you produce measurable results and create the life you want instead of living day to day with unfulfilled dreams. Be Smart Girls knows that managing stress (and yes, life will always create stress) is the number one way to encourage productivity and efficiency.

At Be Smart Girls, we know that some people have more money than others, some have more education, and others have more skills, but when it comes to time, we are all on the same playing field. We all have 24 hours in a day, 168 hours in a week, and so on. What you do or don't do in this time determines your success in life. By providing information, tips, and real-life stories, Be Smart Girls can make you more focused, more productive, and make your time ... TIME WELL SPENT.

Be Smart Girls understands the fear of change. We will guide you step by step through the process of changing from a hectic, stressful, unsatisfying life to one that is filled with joy and prosperity. If you commit to using the goal setting and time management skills taught in this book, you will see amazing results.

As long as you're going to think anyway—you might as well think BIG!
—Donald Trump

How to Use This Book

We at Be Smart Girls were inspired to write this book by the many clients we have helped achieve success. This book is composed of some of our best tips and techniques. To illustrate our concepts and to assist you with your exercises, we have provided real-life experiences of actual clients (names have been changed to protect the innocent). We would like to introduce our Be Smart Girls savvy businesswoman, Lindsey. Wherever you see Lindsey's picture, you will find helpful tips to assist you in getting the most out of your day.

Lindsey

Place she calls home: New York City

Career choice: VP of Operations

Hobbies: Jogging, going to the theater, playing mah-jongg

Style: Sophisticated, but not too stuffy

Mantra: "It's the start that stops you, so get moving!"

We felt that our book had to be interactive, so we have incorporated assignments throughout the chapters. We have found from working with our clients that unless they were tasked with an assignment, they seldom took action. Being organized is a learned skill, and by following along in this book and participating in the exercises, you will soon LEARN just how easy it is to transform your life.

Please feel free to write in this book on the pages marked **Assignment**. However, we know many will choose not to mark the pages, so we have provided extra assignment forms at the back of the book for you to copy and use as needed.

Be Smart Girls (BSG) has incorporated icons throughout the book to assist you in accomplishing your goals.

Think of these icons as a call to action.

 The Assignment Icon: Stop reading and complete the assignment that we have outlined for you. It is essential that you complete these assignments because organizing is a learned skill. The Be Smart Girls assignments have taught many of our clients to be organized and stay organized.

The Timer Icon: Set a timer or an alarm, or just check your watch. Tasks won't seem as daunting if you have an established end-time. Be Smart Girls has estimated the time it will take you to complete each assignment.

The Planner Icon: Follow the directions provided where you see this icon and schedule the task into your daily calendar as instructed. Be Smart Girls knows the importance of writing down tasks and scheduling time to complete them.

The End-of-Assignment Icon: When you see this, you know you have reached the end of an assignment. Continue reading, or take a break. Just remember to schedule time to come back to your book. It is important to keep your momentum, so don't let too much time pass.

Tell me and I forget.
Teach me and I remember.
Involve me and I learn.
—Benjamin Franklin

It is essential to follow the Be Smart Girls guidelines to reach your goals.

What does being disorganized cost us?

- It costs more than just time. We all know the saying "Time is money!" Twenty percent of a disorganized person's workday is spent looking for things. As the employer, you are paying workers to find stuff, rather than for working. As the employee, you are working late without financial gain to complete tasks that should have been done during the standard workday.

- The average person spends two hours of their day looking for misplaced items. Think about how you would choose to spend two hours of free time. There is your incentive to get organized!

- It costs us emotionally when we are too stressed out from our day to spend quality time with our family and friends. Clutter invokes feelings of discontent and stress.

- It costs us physically when we can't find the time to cook healthy meals or to participate in an exercise program.

What does it mean to be organized?

- It means finding what you need, when you need it.

- It means not having to hunt around for hours looking for something you are sure you had a minute ago.

- It means presenting yourself in the best light to your boss and co-workers.

- It means realizing your goals and dreams!

Chapter One:
Time Management

- Do you let time control you?

- Conquer the ticking clock, and you will have less stress and be more productive.

- Plan and organize your day in time increments.

- Schedule uninterrupted time to focus on important projects.

Lose an hour in the morning, and you will spend all day looking for it.
—*Richard Whately*

We would like to introduce you to our client Erika, who came to us overwhelmed, overworked, and unproductive.

Erika worked for a well-known investment firm as a financial analyst. She had recently been demoted from a private office to a cubicle. The firm's operating guidelines rewarded employees who achieved high productivity with private offices. It is quite common in many industries, including real estate, financial advising, and sales, to use productivity as an incentive for assigning office space.

During our initial consultation with Erika, we found she was working long hours but still not accomplishing her sales goals. At Be Smart Girls, we know longer hours do not directly correlate to increased productivity.

We asked Erika to describe her workload and found that she had an endless to-do list. As a result, Erika was paralyzed. Does this sound familiar? The mental clutter made even the simplest task seem daunting. She spent much of her time avoiding her tasks, talking to co-workers, trying to determine where to start, feeling hopeless, and just being overwhelmed.

We have all been trained to write to-do lists but not how to use them efficiently. In chapter two, we will demonstrate the effectiveness of prioritized to-do lists and task scheduling to maximize your productivity.

 **Assignment** **Task time: 15 minutes**

Estimating productivity

Answer the following questions: (Be honest, we can't see your answers.)

- How many days per week do you work? _____
- How many hours per day? _____
- Do you work overtime (more than 40 hours per week)? _____
- Estimate what percentage of your day you are productive. _____

Here are Erika's responses

- How many days per week do you work? <u>5 to 6 days</u>
- How many hours per day? <u>10 hours</u>
- Do you work overtime (more than 40 hours per week)? <u>yes</u>
- Estimate what percentage of your day you are productive. <u>96%</u>

Ninety-six percent! We had to inform Erika that her self-assessed productivity results did not correlate with her actual productivity. Given that she had the technical training and skills to excel at her job, as proven by past performance, at 96 percent efficiency, she would be achieving the company's sales quota and would not have lost her private office.

To get a more accurate picture of how Erika actually spent her time, we asked her to record her daily tasks, indicate the amount of time spent on each task, and add up the total time spent. An example of Erika's Task Sheet can be found later in this chapter. We then worked with her to evaluate the results of this exercise.

 Assignment *Task time: 15 minutes*

Using the Task Sheet provided later in this chapter

- **Write** down your daily tasks in the first column. We suggest you visualize a typical day in your office, or better yet, write down the tasks you completed yesterday. The key for this assignment is to get something down on paper. Think of it like a food diary where you must record everything you eat. You must record everything you do and how much time it takes you to do it.

- **Calculate** the approximate time it takes to complete each task and record it in column 2.

- **Add** all the numbers in column 2 to get your total time spent per day. This will provide an accurate calculation of how you spend your day and make you more conscious of where you can improve. Track your results for at least 2 days, preferably a week.

- **Evaluate** each task by weighing the benefits in comparison to the time it takes to complete it. You may realize that you are not working efficiently and may find it in your best interest to delete a task or two. Sometimes we do things out of habit rather than necessity.

Contact management tips from Lindsay:

- Don't write on scraps of paper.

- Put all phone numbers in a Rolodex, your planner, or contact manager (MS Outlook). Consider purchasing a card scanner.

- Staple business cards to file cards in your Rolodex instead of rewriting the information.

- Use plastic sleeves to insert business cards into your day planner.

- Sort business contacts quarterly to remove obsolete numbers and contacts.

- Keep a spiral-bound notebook next to your phone and record all phone messages and notes in one place instead of using Post-it Notes or scraps of paper.

Erika's Task Sheet	
Task	**Time to Complete**
Filing	30 minutes
Answering e-mails	60 minutes
Preparing for meetings	120 minutes
Lunch	60 minutes
Breaks	30 minutes
Checking voice mail	15 minutes
Returning phone calls	90 minutes
Running errands	60 minutes
Picking up clients from airport	90 minutes
Making to-do lists	30 minutes
Drafting proposals	30 minutes
Total Time Spent per Day	10 hours, 15 minutes

Task Sheet	
Task	Time to Complete
Total Time Spent per Day	

As a result of this simple activity, Erika saw that she was wasting more time than she originally thought. Erika was relieved to realize that it was her time management skills that were holding her back, not her capabilities. On a positive note, time management is a skill that we were able to teach her. After we taught Erika the Be Smart Girls guidelines and techniques discussed in this chapter, she began to see immediate results, and so will you.

Lindsey wants to know: Do you let time control you? She suggests you ...

- Conquer the ticking clock, and you will have less stress and be more productive.

- Plan and organize your day in time increments.

- Schedule uninterrupted time to focus on important projects.

Be Smart Girls time management 101

Be Smart Girls train themselves to think of projects as a series of smaller tasks that need to be completed within a given time frame to meet the project deadline. These tasks need to be scheduled on your daily calendar. Think of each task as you would if you needed to go to the dentist. First, you call the dentist's office to make the appointment, and then you schedule the date and time in your calendar or planner. Lastly, you show up at the appointed time and complete the task by seeing the dentist. Your tasks need to be processed the same way. Schedule appointments with yourself, and show up mentally prepared to accomplish the tasks at the time you assigned to complete them.

Let's take a look at some of Erika's daily tasks:

Checking e-mail	Lunch break
Returning phone calls	Going to post office
Preparing for meetings	Making a to-do list
Checking voice mail	Picking up client from the airport
Getting mail	Filing
Coffee break	Working on proposal

Although it is helpful to have a list of daily tasks, that in itself will not ensure that you will find the time in the day to complete them. Be Smart Girls has developed a way to prevent endless to-do lists. Be Smart Girls knows that simple to-do lists lack the vital main ingredient: a time table in which to accomplish them. This is similar to a recipe that lists all the ingredients but is missing the measurements.

 Assignment   *Task time: 30 minutes*

Using the Daily Calendar

With your daily tasks listed, you must make a plan to complete these tasks. Using the Daily Calendar we have provided, schedule all tasks at the time allotted to them each day. Even if it is just a five-minute phone call or ten minutes talking to a co-worker, we want you to write it down.

Be Smart Girls tip

If you have an out-of-office meeting, make sure you factor in the time it takes to commute and park when allocating time in your schedule for the meeting. For example: Erika has a meeting that has a ten-minute commute time each way. The meeting itself is thirty minutes, so Erika needs to schedule fifty to sixty minutes for the meeting, or her schedule will be off, causing overlapping of appointments.

Busy versus productive

At Be Smart Girls, we recognize the difference between being busy and being productive. There is an important distinction between the two. You can literally be busy every moment of your day, but that doesn't necessarily mean that you have been productive. At BSG we define busy as being constantly in motion, frenetically running around, stressed to the limit, and doing things at ninety miles an hour. At the end of the day, you are exhausted and maybe even proud of what you have done. But what do you really have to show for it? Did the tasks you accomplished have to be completed by someone at your skill level, by someone holding your job title? If you were hired as the marketing manager making $65,000 per year, the company expects you to focus on tasks that must be done by someone of your skill level. Does it help the company if you spend your time running copies? Could this task be done by someone making $25,000 a year? It is easy to fall into the trap of being busy, spending your time checking off all the low-level tasks on your to-do list. Being productive means focusing on the tasks that correspond to your skill level. As a manager, you must learn to delegate tasks according to the skill level required to complete them. Empower your staff to assist you instead of micromanaging.

If you are a small-business owner, you realize you must wear many hats. Even though you are the CEO, you may also be the bookkeeper, receptionist, and customer service rep. You need to prioritize your day so that you focus on the most critical issues first if you want your company to move forward. You may need to hire a part-time assistant to handle some of the entry-level tasks, such as preparing mailings, ordering office supplies, and answering the phone. You may consider enlisting your children's help to stuff envelopes or file documents.

Remember: Focus on being productive, not busy.

Daily Calendar	Today's Date: 01/02/2007
7:00	Arrive at work, check e-mail, and respond
7:45	Prepare for 8:00 meeting
8:00	Meeting
9:00	Check voice mail
9:15	Return phone calls, filing
10:00	Coffee break, quick walk around office building
10:15	Meeting
11:15	Work on proposal
12:00	Lunch break
1:00	Drive to post office, pick up mail
1:30	Drive to airport, park, wait for client to arrive
2:00	Drive client to office
2:30	Meeting
3:00	Coffee break, talk to co-workers
3:15	Work on proposal
4:00	End-of-day filing
4:45	Prepare to-do list for tomorrow, organize desk
5:00	Leave work

Daily Calendar	Today's Date: _____
7:	
8:	
9:	
10:	
11:	
12:	
1:	
2:	
3:	
4:	
5:	

Lindsey's advice on meetings:

You can have fewer meetings and be more productive if you follow these guidelines:

- Limit the time for meetings.
- Have a written agenda.
- Set a timer to alert you 15 minutes before your scheduled time to meet.
- Ask participants to come prepared with notepads, pens, etc.
- Keep to the topic.
- Assign action tasks with deadlines at the conclusion of the meeting.

Lindsey suggests that you use a planner:

- Buy an organizer or planner, or use an electronic version.
- Customize it to fit your specific needs.
- Keep all appointments, tasks, prioritized to-do lists, etc. in one place.
- Combining work, family, and personal items on one calendar prevents over-scheduling and missed appointments.
- Keep it easily accessible.
- Consider buying a smart phone to combine your cell phone and electronic planner.

Chapter Two:
Project Management

- Stop multitasking and start single tasking for increased productivity.

- Break projects into manageable tasks, and assign incremental completion deadlines.

- Use the Be Smart Girls Daily Priority Charts to manage your projects and time.

Tasks that are "hard by the yard"
often become a relative
"cinch by the inch".
—Unknown

You often hear people brag about their ability to do several things at a time. Being able to do something and doing it well are two different things.

Many people believe that when they multitask, they will get more done in less time. But Be Smart Girls knows that this is not true. Research shows that when people multitask, they reduce productivity, and the quality of their work decreases. Research documented in the August 2005 issue of *The Journal of Experimental Psychology: Human Perception and Performance* revealed that for all types of tasks, subjects lost time when they had to switch from one task to another, and time costs increased with the complexity of the task. Time costs were also greater when subjects switched to tasks they weren't very familiar with.

Take Brooke, for example. Brooke worked for an ad agency and found herself always running behind on assignments and missing deadlines. Brooke prided herself on being a great multitasker. Brooke would sit at her computer researching one project while completing another, answer her phone when it rang, get interrupted by co-workers, and eat her lunch—all at the same time. Even though she was working on a tight deadline, Brooke looked up the phone number to the pizza joint down the road for Ted when he came in looking for lunch ideas. She picked up her ringing phone and spent fifteen minutes talking to a salesperson about something Brooke neither needs nor has the authority to buy on behalf of the company. All of this while she checked to see whether she got an e-mail from her girlfriend regarding dinner plans after work. Can you relate?

As 4:00 PM approached, Brooke was nowhere near the completion of her project. She was stressed and out of time. When her boss stopped by to check on the status of the project, Brooke explained that she didn't even take a break for lunch, she hadn't moved from her office, and she had been working on her project the whole time. Perception and reality were not in alignment with each other. Bottom line, Brooke should have been single tasking like a smart girl rather than multitasking. You are more productive when you focus on one task for a predetermined amount of time instead of jumping from subject to subject.

Brooke needed to ...

- **Set** an appointment with herself to work on her top priority project until it was completed.

- **Inform** her coworkers that she was on a deadline

Multitasking has become a way of life. But Lindsey knows that you get more done if you concentrate on just one thing at a time.

- Use the power of focus.

- Even 15 minutes of uninterrupted time can produce amazing resuts.

and should not be interrupted unless there was a fire in the building.

Be Smart Girls knows that with today's demands we cannot completely eliminate multitasking, but we can help you restructure your day and tasks to make you more productive and efficient.

Project management

When tackling a project, it is common to make a to-do list and complete the easy things first, leaving important tasks to linger until crunch time, resulting in missed deadlines. To-do lists have a purpose; however, to use them effectively, you have to prioritize.

3-step process for prioritizing tasks

1. **Break** the project into smaller, more manageable tasks.
2. **Record** all tasks in order of importance using the BSG Priority Chart (provided in the forms section).
3. **Schedule** tasks in the BSG Daily Calendar, allotting the time required to complete them (forms section).

To do two things at once is to do neither.
—Publilius Syrus

Every day you have to make choices based on your work-load. We will teach you how to use the BSG Daily Priority Chart to guide you productively through your day. At the end of each day, establish your priorities for the next day. Plan ahead.

Lindsey's prioritizing tips:

- **Use** 15 minutes each day to plan your day, review your tasks, and fill in your BSG Daily Calendar and BSG Priority Chart for the next day.

- **Preplan.** If you know something needs to be done on Friday, don't wait until Friday to schedule it for completion. Be proactive and plan ahead. Advanced planning allows you to get an early start each day.

- **Don't** give up. It takes ONLY 21 days to create a new habit.

- **Break** projects into smaller, manageable tasks. Accomplishing tasks in increments gives you a sense of accomplishment and keeps you on schedule.

Miscalculating the amount of time it takes to do something is a common mistake and can be discouraging. Energy levels are a contributing factor. Over time, you will be able to determine when you have the most energy and will realize that to increase your productivity you must schedule your difficult tasks during this period.

Brooke's Daily Priority Chart   Date: 03/05/07

Priority 1 Tasks MUST DO Today (accomplish during most productive time of day)	Complete (x)
Proofread McKenzie brochure	
Contact ABC Printing for price quote for Taylor	
Return call to business prospect Lawson Insurance	
Priority 2 Tasks SHOULD DO Today (not until Priority 1 Tasks have been completed)	Complete (x)
E-mail Lydia regarding the fall line	
Get final approval on proof of Taylor's print ad	
Meet with accounting to review expense report	

Priority 3 Tasks WOULD LIKE TO DO Today (not at the expense of Priority 1 or 2 Tasks)	Complete (x)
Research women's networking group	
Check into advanced computer training course	

Assignment *Task time: 20 minutes*

List all the projects you are responsible for

Be Smart Girls wants you to consider this list in terms of priority.

- Priority 1 (RED) tasks are those you must accomplish today and should do so during your most productive hours.

- Priority 2 (YELLOW) tasks are those you should do today but not until Priority 1 tasks have been completed.

- Priority 3 (BLUE) tasks are those that you would like to do today but not at the expense of Priority 1 and 2 tasks.

Take the list and put the word RED next to the tasks that are Priority 1.
Write YELLOW next to the tasks that are Priority 2.
Write BLUE next to your tasks that are Priority 3.

Using the BSG Daily Priority Chart, transfer your prioritized tasks into the appropriate section of the color-coded chart. Using the BSG Daily Calendar, schedule time to complete your now-prioritized tasks (found in the Forms section). In time, you will be able to determine when you are at your best and schedule difficult tasks accordingly.

Apply the principles we have taught you and incorporate the BSG Daily Priority Chart and BSG Daily Calendar into your daily routine. This will improve your efficiency and increase your productivity.

Daily Priority Chart   Date: _____

Priority 1 Tasks MUST DO Today (accomplish during most productive time of day)	Complete (x)
Priority 2 Tasks SHOULD DO Today (not until Priority 1 Tasks have been completed)	Complete (x)
Priority 3 Tasks WOULD LIKE TO DO Today (not at the expense of Priority 1 or 2 Tasks)	Complete (x)

and her friends met for drinks after work. Most of her friends grew tired of hearing the same old complaints from her: "not enough money," "hates her boss," "hates her old car," "wants to lose twenty pounds," and on and on. Nicole's complaints never changed because she didn't change her focus. Nicole was just idly going through her days, months, and years without a plan of action. At Be Smart Girls, we know that it is important to have goals, put them in writing, and set timelines for their completion. Nicole was defeated before she even began, because she didn't have a plan. Nicole did have one thing going for her: her discontent; having the desire for change is the first step towards achieving it.

We asked Nicole to take fifteen minutes to make a list of things she would like to accomplish with her life (career, family, home, self, finances). We told her they could be as basic or dynamic as she wanted. At first, she had a hard time thinking of something. We told her to take her time, and soon she had a list compiled that she was excited about. Next to each goal we had her create a deadline, a period in which she planned to accomplish these goals. This would help her reach her goals.

Nicole's Goals	Time
Create a phone log	1 week
Increase clientele	1 month
Make more money	1 year

Buy a new car	4 months
Lose weight	3 months
Learn Spanish	1 year
Travel to Europe	6 months
Start own business	2 years
Create a dream board	2 weeks
Buy a new home	3 years

 Assignment **Task time: 15 minutes**

Setting your goals

In fifteen minutes, write ten to twenty things you want to do, have, or be. If you need more space, use the extra forms in the Forms section of this book. Remember: your goals can be as lofty or simple as you wish. Just write whatever comes to your mind. You can always edit them. Next to each goal create a timeline, a period in which you would like to accomplish these goals.

Short: 1 to 4 weeks; **Moderate:** 1 to 6 months; **Long:** 6 months or longer

Goal	Time

Be Smart Girls goal setting tips:

- **Put** all goals in writing and reevaluate along the way.

- **Break down** long-term goals into a series of moderate- and short-term goals.

- **Prioritize** tasks to be completed.

- **Schedule** time to accomplish your goals.

- **Reward** yourself for incre- mental accomplishments.

- **Create** a dream board. You  can include personal and business photos of board rooms, office buildings, cars, helping others, a fit body, and vacation destinations as a motivation for obtaining your goals.

- **Take Action!** Make a commitment to your- self and start today!

Now that you have identified your goals, we will show you examples and provide assignments so you can make your goals a reality.

Short-term goal

One of Nicole's short-term goals was to create a phone log for recording all phone messages and follow-up items. We asked Nicole to respond to the following:

List 3 reasons for not accomplishing this goal yet:

- Not sure how.
- Need supplies.
- Procrastination.

Write why you feel you need to complete the goal or what the benefit is of completing this task:

- Save time. All information will be in one place instead of having to look through scraps of paper and Post-it Notes.
- Won't lose important contact numbers.
- Feel more in control if information is easily accessible.

What steps will you take to complete this goal?

- Buy a notebook.
- Write down calls in the notebook.
- Find a place to keep my newly created phone log for easy retrieval.

Now that Nicole has written down the steps needed to complete this goal, she has to schedule time to complete them. She must put the task of buying the notebook on her BSG Daily Priority Chart and then schedule the time in her BSG Daily Calendar to go to the office supply store. Nicole must continue this process until she has scheduled time for each part of the process.

Only by scheduling actions with yourself will you accomplish them. Treat these appointments as you would a doctor's appointment. You wouldn't miss the doctor's appointment, so treat yourself with the same respect. Get in the mind-set that you will accomplish your tasks at the time you assigned.

 *Assignment*   *Task time: 30 minutes*

Select a short-term goal: It is best to start by selecting and accomplishing a short-term goal. This sense of accomplishment will give you the positive energy needed to keep reaching for your goals and realizing your dreams. Remember that long-term goals, although they may seem impossible, are just a series of short-term goals. Thinking of them in this light makes them seem more achievable.

Respond to the following

Choose a short term goal from your list: _____

List 3 reasons for not accomplishing this goal yet.

-
-
-

Write why you feel you need to complete the goal or what the benefit is of completing this task.

-
-
-

What steps will you take to complete this goal?

-
-
-

 Schedule time to complete the necessary steps in your BSG Daily Calendar and BSG Daily Priority Chart.

Did you complete the assignment? How does it feel to have accomplished one of your goals? Apply the principles we have taught you to all the goals on your list. With your new sense of achievement, you are now ready to tackle your moderate goals.

Moderate goal

Nicole's moderate goal was to increase her clientele.

List 3 reasons for not accomplishing this goal yet:

- Not organized.
- Fear of rejection.
- Not sure how to do it.

Write why you feel you need to complete the goal or what the benefit is of completing this task:

- Increase business.
- Make more money.
- Help more people.

What steps will you take to complete this goal?

- Read a book on the subject.
- Take SCORE workshop (www.score.org).
- Join a networking group.

 Assignment   *Task time: 30 minutes*

Select a moderate-term goal: Applying the same principles that you used to accomplish your short-term goal, break your moderate goal into smaller tasks. Don't be intimidated; we know you can do it. The goal is to keep your momentum moving forward.

Respond to the following:

Choose a moderate-term goal from your list: _____

List 3 reasons for not accomplishing this goal yet.

-
-
-

Write why you feel you need to complete the goal or what the benefit is of completing this task.

-
-
-

What steps will you take to complete this goal?

-
-
-

Schedule time to complete the necessary steps in your BSG Daily Calendar and BSG Daily Priority Chart.

Did you complete the assignment? How does it feel to have accomplished one of your moderate goals? Apply the principles we have taught you to all the goals on your list. With your new sense of achievement, you are now ready to tackle your long-term goals.

Long-term goal

Nicole's long-term goal was to buy a new home.

List 3 reasons for not accomplishing this goal yet:

- No down payment saved.
- Fear of mortgage commitment.
- Haven't made the time to research locations.

Write why you feel you need to complete the goal or what the benefit is of completing this task:

- Investment rather than spending money on rent.
- Satisfying the dream of owning a home.
- Have my own yard to grow a garden.

What steps will you take to complete this goal?

- Create a dream board (instructions at the end of this chapter).
- Find a real estate agent.
- Create a financial plan for saving down payment.

It is easy to lose sight of long-term goals because the reward seems so far in the future. Many of us live in the here and now and don't plan for the future. By following the Be Smart Girls guidelines, you can make your dreams a reality.

Here is an example of how to break down a long-term goal

Nicole and her husband wanted to buy a house. One of the steps they needed to take to achieve this goal was to set money aside for a down payment. To do this, they needed a plan. To start, they needed to ask themselves these questions:

- What is the top price we are willing to pay? $300,000
- When do we want to buy the home?   3 years (36 months)
- How much do we need for the deposit? 10%

They wanted to buy a $300,000 home in three years and planned on putting 10 percent down. Let's do the math:

$300,000 × 10% = $30,000 required down payment
$30,000 - $10,000 from savings = $20,000 still needed for down payment
$20,000 ÷ 36 months = $555.55 per month

Is this achievable? Be realistic. Don't set yourself up for failure. If it is not possible to save $556 per month, then Nicole and her husband need to look for a less expensive home, extend their time frame, or look for creative home-financing options. Nicole and her husband found that they were able to save an extra $556 per month if they made a few concessions, such as cutting down on eating out, shopping for clothes, and going to the movies. They had to evaluate each decision based on their true desire to obtain their goal of owning a home. They had to ask themselves: Do we really need another camera? Could we pack our lunches rather than eat out? Instead of spending this money, they put their savings in an account earmarked for the down payment on their home.

Each day remind yourself of your goals and make sure your actions match them. If you really want them and are truly committed, all of your goals can be achieved.

 Assignment *Task time: 30 minutes*

Select a long-term goal: Applying the same principles that you used to accomplish your short- and moderate-term goals, break your long-term goal into smaller tasks.

Don't be intimidated; we know you can do it. The goal is to keep your momentum moving forward.

Respond to the following

Choose a long-term goal from your list: _____

List 3 reasons for not accomplishing this goal yet.

-
-
-

Write why you feel you need to complete the goal or what the benefit is of completing this task.

-
-
-

What steps will you take to complete this goal?

-
-
-

Schedule time to complete the necessary steps in your BSG Daily Calendar and BSG Daily Priority Chart.

Did you complete the assignment? How does it feel to have accomplished one of your long-term goals? Apply the principles we have taught you to all the goals on your list.

What is a dream board, and how do you create one?

A dream board is a visual representation of your goals. It is created with a collection of pictures and words that represent your goals, such as a dream house, a dream car, a corner office, places you want to travel to, and quotes and sayings that inspire or describe you.

Our dreams are our incentives for getting up in the morning and going to work.

Supplies:
Magazines
Googleimages.com (to search and print the images you want)
Glue stick
Poster board

Be creative and customize your board to fit your personality. You can pin your photos on a bulletin board, place them in a frame, or simply paste them on poster paper in a collage. Hang your dream board in a place you can view daily. Start and end each day by looking at your dream board and visualizing what your life will be like when your dreams have become a reality.

The key is to give yourself a visual represention and reminder of your goals. **Dream big! If you believe it, you can achieve it.**

Chapter Four:
Desk a Disaster

- A clear desk allows for a more productive work space.

- Limit your pictures and mementos to no more than three items. Keep an open work area.

- Remember to clear your desk at the end of each day. Just 15 minutes will allow you to start fresh the next day.

Life asks us to make measurable progress in reasonable time. That's why they make those fourth-grade chairs so small.
—*Jim Rohn*

At Be Smart Girls, we stress the importance of controlling your physical environment. Now that we have dealt with mental clutter in chapter one, you need to deal with physical clutter (your office, your desk, etc.).

When we first met Marla, she was stressed out and too embarrassed to even show us her office. Instead, she met us in the conference room and tried to explain what she was dealing with. One of her co-workers came by and exclaimed, "Marla! So glad to see you in here. I just went by your office and couldn't find you. I thought you might be buried, so I called the Search and Rescue Team." As the laughter faded down the hallway, Marla, beet red, looked at us and shrugged. We asked Marla what area in her office was causing her the most stress and adding to her decreased productivity. In some cases, it may be a person's desk; in others, it's the credenza; and still others, it's the filing cabinet. Marla said she wanted to begin with the top of her desk that was piled high with paper.

Before we begin clearing your office, we need you to gather the supplies needed.

 Assignment *Task time: 30 minutes*

Getting Supplies: Get one plastic or cardboard box for each use listed below (we use the words "boxes" and "bins" interchangeably). Choose the one that best suits your needs. Just make sure the containers have lids because you may need to stack them.

Supplies and their intended uses

Trash can: Obvious trash.

Shred bin: Sensitive documents to be destroyed. Please adhere to company, accounting, and industry-specific guidelines. (If you have a large amount, consider hiring a local, bulk-document destruction company.)

Recycle bin: Expired notices, circulars, invitations, and nonsensitive paper.

Paper bin: Paper you are keeping for sorting later. Refer to paper handling section in chapter five.

Home bin: Personal items that belong at home.

Donate bin: Items you want to give to charity.

Office supply closet bin: Overstocked items that need to be returned to the office supply closet.

Be Smart Girls tips for getting started:

- Block out dedicated time for this project.

- Play upbeat music for motivation.

- Have snacks and water handy. Don't give yourself an excuse to get sidetracked.

- Stay on task. Do not answer the phone.

- If you're decluttering your home office, make sure the kids are cared for, etc.

- If you're working at your business office, let the receptionist know to hold your calls, or come in on a nonwork day or after hours.

- Each session should be a minimum of 2 hours until the project is completed.

- Keep your momentum going.

At this time, we are going to have you do a bulk sort. This allows you to clear your space. We will show you how to process each category or box later. Right now, we want you to see results.

 **Assignment** *Task time: 2-hour sessions*

1. **Clear** a space on the floor for safe standing and maneuverability.

2. **Remove** all items off your desk except for the computer, phone, and other electronics (printer, etc.) that are connected. A clear desk also gives you a clean work space for sorting papers.

3. **Knickknacks:** Although your knickknacks and family photos may seem necessary, at Be Smart Girls we recommend limiting your personal effects to one or two items. When you have a menagerie, it actually contributes to clutter instead of creating the effect you had intended. Put all excess items in a bin designated for its final destination, such as home, donate, or office-supply closet.

4. **Office supplies:** Sort and purge all office supplies. Keep only a small supply of the items you truly need. You do not need 3 staplers, 6 boxes of paper clips, etc. Place the items you are keeping in your desk drawers. Do not keep them on your desktop because they are not decorations. Even items that you use frequently can be retrieved from a desk drawer and then returned. Place the office supplies you no longer need

in the appropriate bin labeled office-supply closet, donate, or home (if they belong to you and you need them at home).

5. **Old equipment:** Do you have old equipment that you are not using, such as printers, scanners, phones, or calculators, clogging up your desk? If so, now is the time to remove them. Put them in either the donate bin or trash bin if they no longer work.

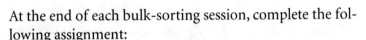

At the end of each bulk-sorting session, complete the following assignment:

 Assignment *Task time: 30 minutes*

Empty donate and office-supply closet bins:

- **Put** the donate bin in your car. Try to drop off donations by the end of the day or within 24 hours. Check your area for local charity drop-off stations, such as Goodwill, the Salvation Army, or St. Vincent de Paul.
- **Put** the office supplies back in the supply closet.

At the end of the project, reward yourself. Have this reward in mind while you are working because it will keep you motivated. Examples of motivating rewards include a manicure, pedicure, or going to a movie. You now have a desk you can be proud of. Enjoy!

Chapter Five:
File Management

- Excess paper can turn into clutter.

- Clutter creates stress.

- Stress leads to lost productivity.

- Buried under too much paper? What happened to the promise that the computer age would bring us a paperless society? We have even more paper now than ever before!

I find that the harder I work, the more luck I seem to have.
—Thomas Jefferson

You will only reference or use 20 percent of the papers, forms, e-mails, and reports that you keep. This is commonly known as the 80/20 principle. That means only 20 percent of what you currently have is needed. Using the Be Smart Girls guidelines we provide, you should be able to eliminate the excess 80 percent. Take a moment to imagine how serene your office would be if you had 80 percent less paper in it. Make this image your incentive for completing your assignments.

Be Smart Girls Guidelines for what to keep and what to throw away

Be extremely critical during this process. Consider the following as you evaluate each piece of paper:

- **Can you get this information somewhere else?** If you printed the information from a Web site, can you find it again using a quick search, adding to your favorites, and/or by saving it electronically? If yes, put in the recycle bin.

- **What is the worst-case scenario if you lost this paper?** Would you be released from your job? Lose a client? Go to prison? If you find the consequence isn't all that serious, then don't keep the paper. Put it in the recycle bin.

- **Keep all action items.** These are items that you must act on. We will teach you how to handle these later in this book.

- **Keep all reference items.** We are referring to one-of-a-kind pieces of paper, something you can't get anywhere else. While doing this, ask yourself: Can I obtain this information from another department in the company? Or another resource? If yes, put it in the recycle bin.

- **Keep historical documents.** If you are going to keep these items, do not keep them in your office filing cabinet. At Be Smart Girls we consider this "prime real estate" and reserve it for active files only. You should archive historical documents. Refer to company, accounting, or industry-specific guidelines to determine what must be kept. For example, if you come across a document dated 1973 and you haven't missed it, that is a good sign it may not be important enough to clutter your space with any longer. Recycle it. Don't laugh. As we stated in the beginning of the book, we are using scenarios from real clients. As you go through this process, ask yourself, "Am I being a Smart Girl? Do I really need this paper?"

- **Limit magazines and catalogs:** Recycle all outdated catalogs and magazines. Be Smart Girls recommends setting a reading time to go through your magazines each week before the next issue arrives. If you are a department head and the information is a must-read, delegate reading assignments to other team or staff members. Have them report the highlights of the articles during weekly meetings. This allows for information sharing and decreases the amount of time dedicated to the interoffice transfer of reading materials (which, let's face it, are rarely read). We have talked to many employees who indicate they rarely have time to read, so they just sign the interoffice envelope and send it to the next person. Most of these magazines never get read. This time-consuming process is inefficient.

Straight-line filing:

At Be Smart Girls, we know the most efficient way to maintain and retrieve your files is to establish a straight-line filing system. A straight-line filing system is set up with all file folders tabs in a straight line, either all on the left, center, or right. This is opposed to the more traditional style of filing, which is to stagger the file folder tabs going from left to right, and then back again.

Straight-line filing has many advantages:

- **It is faster to find the file you are looking for.** Let your fingers do the walking. When looking for a file, all you do is flip through the tabs until you locate the correct one.

- **Easier on your eyes.** Look down a row of labels instead of straining your eyes by forcing them to dart back and forth looking for a file.

- **Effortless to maintain.** Unlike traditional filing when your system would come to a halt if you did not have the appropriate file to complete the sequence, the straight-line filing system is simple. Purchase straight-line files, and when you need to add a new file, all you have to do is label it and insert it into the system.

- **More economical.** How many times have you purchased a box of assorted file folders only to find out you have an overabundance of middle-, right-, or left-tabbed folders? With straight-line filing, you will use all of your folders because you do not have to worry about following a sequence.

Before we take you through the process of sorting and filing your documents, you need to gather the necessary supplies. Be Smart Girls knows the importance of being prepared.

 Assignment   *Task time: 30 minutes*

Supplies you need for this project

- Manila file folders
- Pencil

- Standard green hanging file folders
- Cardboard file boxes (also referred to as "banker's boxes")

Prepare your supplies

- Assemble two of your banker's boxes.
- Hang several green file folders in the banker's boxes.
- Put a Post-it Note or write on the front of each box, labeling the first box A–K and the second box L–Z.

●━━━━━━━━━━━━━━━━━━━━━━━━━━━●

The purpose of your next exercise is to create temporary files. At Be Smart Girls, we know it is important to create a system for your most current documents first. We don't want you to take time to clean out your old filing system until you have applied the Be Smart Girls guidelines to your most current documents.

While you are sorting through your paper, you may come across a large amount of paper for one particular category. If a category seems to be expanding rapidly, you need to create subcategories. Subcategories make it easier to find and retrieve items at a later date. Be Smart Girls refers to this process as the "quick and easy."

Function over form

Although you may like having beautiful files, you need to have a system that is functional first. You can create temporary files to test your system before you make pretty colored files and spend a lot of time printing labels that you may not need.

Don't make your categories too broad or too specific. The goal for any filing system is quick retrieval. If you have too many files and papers in your filing cabinet, your drawers will be overstuffed and inefficient. We often find that clients stack papers to be filed on top of their cabinets because the system is at its maximum capacity or they have created a system that is too hard to follow. Keep it simple.

Lindsey's filing tips:

- Use straight-line filing.

- Label a hanging folder for each category using 3½-inch file tabs. This will allow for a descriptive file name.

- Use manila or colored file folders inside the hanging folder.

- Do NOT remove the hanging folders when pulling files because this allows you to easily return files to their correct home after use.

To get you started, we have made a list of some commonly used categories and subcategories.

Prospects	Bob Allen
	Karen Baker
	John Fisher
	Mary Hall
Clients	Katie Albright
	Mark Paxton
	Jenny Wagner
Networking Groups	BNI
	NAFE
Marketing	Web site
	Brochures
	Trade show
Advertising	Newspaper
	Yellow Pages
Forms	Vacation Request Form
	Expense Reports

Sales Invoices (can be filed by month or company)	Jan, Feb, Mar, Apr
Vendors	Susie's Floral
	Flower Power
	Tully's Tulips
To Do	
To Read	Newsletters
	Company literature
Contacts (until they can be recorded in address book)	

Looking at that mountain of papers you plan to keep, reevaluate the necessity of keeping them. We know that you have not been as critical as you would have been if we were sitting next to you.

To assist you, we have created a quick reference guide of the Be Smart Girls Guidelines on What to Keep and What to Throw Away in the Forms section of this book. Make a copy for handy reference while sorting and purging your papers.

Now let's get started with the bin of papers we had you fill in the Desk a Disaster section of chapter four. No matter how many boxes you have, we will help you get through them. Start with just one, preferably the one holding the most recent documents.

 Assignment   *Task time: 2- to 3-hour sessions*

Paper handling

Evaluate each piece of paper. In Desk a Disaster, you should have already eliminated all expired invitations, circulars, and notices. If you do come across such items while sorting, make sure to discard them because they are no longer relevant.

If you know what your categories are in advance, you can begin making your temporary files by writing the name of the category on the manila folders. Take these folders and place them in alphabetical order in the green hanging folders of the banker's boxes that we had you prepare earlier. As you come across a piece of paper that belongs in a category, place the paper in the corresponding manila folder. Continue this process until your pile has diminished, creating new folders as needed. Place all action items (things that need your attention) in a folder marked TO-DO. We will later show you how to use tickler systems for effective handling of your TO-DO folder.

If you are unsure of what categories you may need, don't worry, you can create them as you process each paper. A Be Smart Girls guideline is to create categories based on where you think you would look for that item while trying to retrieve it. For example, it may make more sense for you to retrieve your insurance policy from a file marked with the insurance company's name, such as Allstate. Someone else may search for this document under the type of insurance, such as workers' comp or liability.

The key is to put the item where you are sure to find it when you need it. Continue this process until you have met either your allotted time or have completed your goal, whether that was to complete a whole box or just a stack of papers. We know that this is an exhausting process, but at Be Smart Girls, we know that this is also an essential process and that no one can do it better than you. Stay motivated, set incremental goals, and soon you will have the office of your dreams. OK, maybe it is not the corner office overlooking the ocean, but it will have less clutter, and you will be able to retrieve your documents quickly and easily.

Assignment *Task time: 2- to 3-hour sessions*

Purge old files from existing filing system

- Apply the same process you followed while reviewing your stacks of paper. Always keep in mind that the only reason to keep a document is if you will need it at a future date and there is no other reasonable source for retrieving this document. If you come across items that need your attention, place them in your TO-DO folder.

- If you have not referenced the file in 6 months or longer, apply the 80/20 rule.

File system maintenance

Run maintenance on your file system at least once a quarter, purging items you no longer need. This will free up file space for more relevant documents.

Electronic filing

With improvements made to the scanner and the development of paperless software programs, electronic filing is becoming mainstream. Many companies are moving toward a paperless or semi-paperless environment.

The advantages

- **Easy-to-access files.** Electronic files are set up similar to paper files. Subfolders can be created within main folders. Some people find it easier to use categories such as "Clients" with subfolders consisting of clients' names. Others prefer to use the A–Z method, filing alphabetically. Just like filing with manila folders, use the method that works best for you. The most important key is easy retrieval.

- **The ability to share files.** Shared documents can be stored on a network drive for all employees to access. Confidential documents can be password protected or stored on an individual computer.

- **Reduces paper clutter.** You won't have anymore piles of paper on your desk. All documents that are important enough to keep should be scanned, filed electronically, and then either shredded or recycled.

- **Decreases time spent looking for files.** As we all know, when looking for a paper file, it can be in any number of places. Ideally, it will be correctly filed, but many times it will be on someone else's desk or misfiled. Electronic filing eliminates this time-consuming search. Instead of getting up from your desk and chasing down a file, you can pull it up in an instant.

- **Increases office space by eliminating the need for filing cabinets.** After all of your documents have been scanned and properly filed in your computer, you can free up valuable office space by removing those bulky filing cabinets. Just imagine how much bigger your office could be. With the high cost of commercial real estate, the decision to go paperless is a wise one.

Things to consider

- **Additional training.** You will need to educate yourself and (if applicable) your staff on the fundamentals of operating the scanner, proper filing procedures, and maintaining the system.

- **The initial cost of software and equipment.** If you currently own a scanner, you may consider upgrading. When scanning high volumes of documents, you will need a high-speed scanner to keep your system running efficiently. To assist in file management, invest in a software program such as PaperPort.

- **Tech support for storing and backing up the system.** Now that your files are stored on your computer, you must back up your system. To do this, consult an IT professional. Another consideration is hard drive storage. Depending on the volume, you may need additional storage as the electronic volume grows.

Chapter Six:
Tickler Systems

- Create a system that relies less on memory and more on organization.

- Be Smart Girls knows the importance of having a system for tracking and retrieving tasks and projects.

- Two options: Calendar Tickler System and Priority Tickler System.

To accomplish great things,
we must not only act,
but also dream;
not only plan, but also believe.
—Anatole France

Learning how to manage the constant incoming stream of tasks and projects is the number one way to reduce your stress and increase your productivity. The fear of losing an important document encourages many of us to stack them on our desktops to keep them in sight. The problem is that this results in important papers ending up mixed in with reference papers and even junk mail. Eventually, the piles just keep building on the desk, the filing cabinet, and the floor.

Be Smart Girls knows the importance of having a system for tracking and retrieving tasks and projects. In this chapter, we introduce you to two types of tickler systems: the calendar tickler and the priority tickler. You may prefer one over the other or be served best by using a combination of the two.

Tackling your TO-DO folder

Your most important tasks are now in your TO-DO folder. Assuming you completed the assignments in chapter five. If not, we know you will. We have faith in you and your determination to become a Smart Girl and get organized. By the end of this chapter, you will have a system in place so you never have to worry about forgetting projects.

If you have many small time-sensitive tasks and projects, use the Calendar Tickler System. The Priority Tickler System is another option you can consider, and it works well if your workload is comprised mainly of larger-scale projects.

Calendar Tickler System

Our first tickler system can be described as a "working calendar." The calendar is created with file folders labeled 1–31 for the current month and one hanging file folder for each month marked January through December. This is an efficient system for storing and retrieving items that you must act on instead of searching all over your office for them.

Supply list and use

Desktop file box: To house the tickler system.

Hanging file folders: 15, one for each month in the year (January–December) plus a few extra (consider box-bottom files if standard files won't be sufficient for your workload).

File folders: 31, one for each day of the month.

File labels: Print numbers 1, 2, 3 … to 31 and apply to the monthly files.

Clear 3½-inch plastic tabs: Label January through December and attach to the front of hanging file folders.

Post-it Flags: To mark current day.

How to use the Calendar Tickler System

As you process your TO-DO folder, file each task you plan to complete this month in the folder corresponding to the day you will work on it. You will store ACTION items in the 1–31 folders until you need to act on them. For example, if you have a follow-up call to make on the fifteenth, put the related document in the file marked 15. If you have a report due on the twentieth, and it will take you two days to complete, file it two to three working days before the twentieth. Do not overload any one folder. Be aware that you only have so much time in a day to accomplish your tasks. Only put work in folders corresponding to workdays, skipping weekends and holidays. To make the system efficient, make an entry in your monthly calendar as a reminder of due dates for future tasks.

At the beginning of each workday, pull the file with the number that corresponds with the day's date. Consider these items your assignments for the day. Schedule these items on your BSG Daily Planner, and then act on them.

If you have any items left in the folder at the end of the day, you must reschedule them for another day. Do not automatically put them in the next day's folder. This will create a system where you are never able to complete your daily assignments. You must reevaluate the tasks and the time you have available and set realistic goals by dividing the unfinished work among the actual days you will be able to accomplish it. On a positive note, there is nothing wrong with finishing all the tasks in that day's folder and working ahead on future projects.

At the end of the day, you will move the now-empty folder into the hanging file folder for the following month. For example, at the end of January 1, the file numbered 1 will move into the February hanging folder. (Folders 1–31 are rotating files.)

Having visual files will keep you from over-scheduling. When you see a file is getting too full, move the work to another day. Or if your schedule changes—new meeting or new projects pop up—distribute work scheduled for that day to adjacent open dates.

Tickler system tips:

- Put a copy of a yearly calendar on the front of your desktop file box for easy reference. This makes it easier to determine the day you will work on a project and place it in the correct folder.

- Put the task, action item, or project in the folder for the day you need to act on it, not on the day it is due.

- Make it a habit to pull your daily tickler file at the beginning of each day or at the end of the previous day. Schedule these assignments on your daily planner, and then act on them.

- Keep it visual, and use the tickler system regularly.

- It takes 21 days to form a habit. Commit to checking your system every day. Create a routine for yourself so every day you check your e-mail, voice mail, and then your daily tickler system and to-do lists.

Priority Tickler System

Set up a Priority Tickler System for projects and action items. Using color-coded files, place your TO-DO folders in the appropriate section. For example, if you have a client proposal that must be completed today, place this client's folder in the Red section for immediate attention.

Red (Hot): High-priority or urgent task; complete task immediately
Yellow (Warm): Task needs to be completed soon, but not until Red tasks are done
Blue (Cool): Task needs to be completed, but not until Red and Yellow tasks are done

Accomplish high-priority tasks during the time of the day that you are at your best or have the most energy, such as the first thing in the morning or before lunch. At BSG, we know that when you have a strategy for your day and assign time to complete your tasks, you get more done.

I have learned that we can do anything, but we can't do everything ... at least not at the same time. So think of your priorities not in terms of what activities you do, but when you do them. Timing is everything.
—Dan Millman

Supply list and use

Desktop file box: To house the tickler system.

Hanging file folders: 10 red, 10 yellow, and 10 blue (consider box-bottom files if you have large projects).

File folders: Use manila file folders, instead of color coordinating the folders to hanging files, because the priority of tasks and projects may change, and this will prevent having to change the file folder color. You can just move the file folder to the appropriate colored hanging file folder.

File labels: Print labels identifying projects.

Clear 3½-inch plastic tabs: Print labels HOT priority, WARM priority, COOL priority, and attach to the front of hanging file folders.

How to use the Priority Tickler System

As you process your TO-DO folder, create a file folder for each task or project, and assign it to a priority category. Record the task on your BSG Daily Priority Chart and file it in the corresponding hanging file. You will create a new priority chart each workday. Your HOT priority item must be completed first. Then move on to WARM, and after these are finished, tackle the COOL priority items. Following this system ensures that your most pressing issues get taken care of first. It is all too easy to fall into the trap of accomplishing the easy tasks first while letting bigger tasks slide. It is important to be productive.

Advantages of using tickler systems

- Systems rely less on memory and more on efficiency. Your memory is similar to your computer's hard drive. As it becomes full, it takes longer to retrieve information, and sometimes the system will fail or crash, losing important information.

- Less clutter in office—organized files instead of stacks of paper.

- To-do items are easy to track and retrieve.

 Assignment   *Task time: 60 minutes*

Set up your tickler system:

Determine which of the tickler systems will work best for you. Take sixty minutes to set up your tickler system according to the instructions we have provided. The sooner you begin using a tickler system, the sooner you can control your projects and tasks. Gaining the sense that your workload is manageable and easy to retrieve will clear the mental clutter and allow you to be more productive.

Lindsey asks that you put things away:

- Find a spot for everything, and return it to its spot each time you use it.

- Return borrowed items to your co-workers.

- Take the last 15 minutes of each day to clean up your desk so every morning will be a fresh start.

Chapter Seven: Mail Management

- Sort mail immediately, and do it next to the trash basket and shredder. Only keep what you must. Immediately file papers in your tickler file to act on later or in the appropriate file for future reference. You have already looked at the item, so Do NOT put it in your in-box.

- Be aware that your in-box can become a catchall.

- Respond within 5 days to all correspondence.

- Use e-mail whenever possible because it reduces time spent typing and mailing letters.

- Buy stamps so you can send mail without having to go to the post office.

The most difficult thing is the decision to act, the rest is merely tenacity. The fears are paper tigers. You can do anything you decide to do. You can act to change and control your life; and the procedure, the process is its own reward.
—Amelia Earhart

Do you ever wish that the faithful mailman would take the day or maybe the week off? You may not be able to stop the constant influx of mail, but you can learn how to process it more efficiently. Now that you have your filing system set up, processing mail will be more manageable.

Be Smart Girls Guidelines for processing your mail

- Process it daily.
- Establish a routine. Get your mail at the same time each day and schedule time to process it on your BSG Daily Calendar.
- Process it near your filing system.
- Create a mail processing center with all supplies assembled for daily use.

Supplies for mail processing center

- Trash can
- Shred bin
- Recycle bin
- Calendar to schedule meetings and events
- Postage stamps
- Return address labels
- Pen and pencil

- Desktop file box with hanging file folders labeled: To File, To Do, and To Read (can be combined with desktop tickler system created in previous chapter)

We encourage you to use a desktop file rather than a filing cabinet, at least until following the Be Smart Girls guidelines for processing your mail becomes a habit. Having easy access files encourages you to use them.

Mail processing steps

1. Physically sort through your mail. Immediately discard all junk mail into the recycle bin.

2. Open and process each piece of mail one at a time.

3. Discard outer envelope and unnecessary advertisements.

4. Decide now how to handle each individual piece of mail. File rather than pile. Apply the guidelines established in chapter five: File Management and chapter six: Tickler Systems for efficient paper handling.

5. Use Action folders such as To File, To Do, and To Read for storing mail that will require later action.

   To File: On each piece of paper that you need to file, pencil the name of the file it goes into and the received date in the corner for future filing. Schedule time at the end of each day to file; otherwise before you know it, you will have a huge stack again. Penciling the destination file on each paper allows you to delegate your filing to an assistant, saving you time.

To Do: At Be Smart Girls we prefer that you use your tickler system established in the previous chapter for handling your To Do items. In the event that you chose not to create a tickler system, it is important to have one location for storing and retrieving items that you must act on.

To Read: Items that you want to read at a later date.

6. Schedule all meetings, events, and tickler items on your calendar.

Aside from the faithful mailman, you can also count on your boss and co-workers to fill up your in-box. The same principles and guidelines apply to your in-box as apply to your mail.

Be Smart Girls Guidelines for handling your in-box

- Process it daily.
- Don't use your in-box as a to-do file. Process items by placing them in your tickler system.
- Delegate items or documents to co-workers and staff. Place these items in their in-box for processing.

Lindsey's message on phone calls:

DON'T drop everything to answer the phone unless your job title is receptionist and you are required to do so.

Try to be proactive rather than reactive. Reacting to the requests of others, whether by phone or in person, can eat up a large part of your day in an unproductive manner. Productivity comes from smart choices. Know what needs immediate attention and is worth changing your schedule for, and what can wait. This is a very important lesson to learn.

If possible, establish time in your day for uninterrupted work. Let everyone know that you will only take calls from specific individuals during that time.

Be Smart Girls Guidelines for handling your e-mail and instant messaging

Your e-mail can pile up just as quickly as paper mail. Do you remember when you first discovered e-mail and you were so excited to check your in-box and find one new message? Somebody cared! Now we open our e-mail in-box to find twenty-plus e-mails per day. Some are junk and should quickly be deleted. Others require your action. When you don't process your in-box daily, important e-mails can get buried under new messages as the older ones move to the next page. To handle your e-mail, create an electronic file system similar to the paper version we demonstrated earlier, or print to-do e-mails and incorporate them into your current paper tickler system. Check your e-mail periodically throughout the day. While you need to stay abreast of your incoming e-mails, don't check your in-box every ten seconds as this wastes time. Instead create a system where you check your e-mail first thing in the morning, mid-morning, before lunch, mid-afternoon and then an hour before leaving for the day. This allows you to schedule action items and adjust your daily schedule as required. There are always exceptions; if you are expecting an important e-mail feel free to click that send/receive button until it arrives.

Work within your comfort zone. Don't force yourself to use a system that doesn't fit your style because you won't keep it up. BUT you must have a system! Contrary to what you may believe, an electronic "pile" of e-mails is not a system.

Instant messaging (IMing) is a quick way to respond to co-workers and business associates. Don't get caught up chatting to friends throughout the day. This wastes your time, puts you behind in your work, and contributes to your stress. Be Smart Girls uses both e-mail and instant messaging to send quick messages to co-workers instead of leaving our desks and walking to their offices. By using this convenient technology, we don't waste time or get distracted.

Chapter Eight:
Time for Yourself

- Take a lunch break. Don't eat at your desk or on the run. It creates mess and stress.

- Take a mental break. Walk around the block or around the building to get some fresh air.

- You will find that you are more productive when you return to your desk and the tasks at hand.

They say that time changes things,
but you actually have
to change them yourself.
—Andy Warhol

It is important to take a break. You are using the Be Smart Girls advice, single tasking, and have been working steadily for a couple of hours. You still have a lot to do before you finish your tasks. You are considering working through lunch, but Be Smart Girls knows that you can focus and accomplish more if you take a break.

Instead of powering through your day getting distracted by hunger pains, blurred vision, and restless muscles, schedule some time in the morning and afternoon to address your needs. You will be more productive in the long run. If you don't take a break, you won't completely concentrate on your work. You will make mistakes, fatigue will set in, and you will begin working at a slower pace.

Take Kate, for example. Everyone described Kate as a giver. Without fail, she found time to help almost everyone who asked. Knowing that Kate would say yes, her friends and co-workers often sought her assistance. To accomplish everything she took on, Kate often came to work early, worked through lunch, and was usually one of the last to leave work in the evening. Many times she had to decline fun activities on the weekends to get everything done.

Needless to say, Kate was worn out! Be Smart Girls knows that it is important to take care of yourself first. This is not about being selfish. It is about finding balance and, as such, setting limits on the tasks you take on.

Take the RIGHT break

To replenish your mind, body, and health, concentrate on these three areas:

- **Health:** Schedule snack and/or lunch breaks at the same time every day. Your body will adjust to them. Instead of feeling hungry sporadically throughout the morning, your body will know you will be having a snack around 10:00 AM. Eat healthy, energy-building foods rather than high carb/high sugar foods that will make you fatigued. Have peanut butter on a whole-wheat pita, for instance.

- **Body:** Walk to the restroom, down the hall, to the copy room, or around the building. If you have a home office, take a quick walk to the corner and back. If you have a private office or room, do some stretching exercises. You will find that you can generate renewed energy by moving your body and increasing your blood flow within a few minutes.

- **Mind:** You can take mental breaks when you take exercise breaks. Do yoga breathing while you stretch. Or listen to your favorite music on your MP3 player while you walk. By taking your mind off your work for a brief period of time, you will be able to come back to your desk refreshed.

Make your break mean something. Make it about you and refueling yourself so you feel good and are most productive.

Don't take more than 15 minutes per break.

Don't take more then 2 mini-breaks a day.

Don't skip lunch.

Don't combine work with your break (making copies, answering the phone).

Don't surf the Internet. (You need this time to relax your eyes, relieve mental fatigue, and reduce body strain.)

The main goal for taking a break is to make sure you refuel.

Your mind works better when you have mental clarity, so you need to schedule mini-breaks throughout the work-day to ensure that you keep your mind fresh. This is NOT an invitation to slack off, but instead a pointed way of looking at your time and limiting distractions and writer's block.

Be Smart Girls Guidelines for taking a break

For every two hours worked, take a five-minute break—stand up from your desk, stretch, take a quick walk to get a cup of coffee or bottle of water, or visit the restroom. If you have a window, take a few minutes to look out and notice some detail that will make you feel refreshed when you sit back down at your desk.

Take a lunch break

Many busy people tend to work through their lunch break because they think that they are behind schedule or that they have too much to do to take a lunch. This is counterproductive. You may stay at your desk, the lunch break will come and go, and you still will not have accomplished enough work to justify missing lunch. The brain needs a break. Going to lunch allows you to relieve stress and to come back to your desk refreshed and ready to tackle projects with a fresh outlook. It is also important to replenish your body with food. Eating nourishes the body and gives it energy to continue with your workday.

If you have an hour for lunch, take half the time for eating, and use the other half to take a walk, run an errand, or just relax.

Suggestions for breaks

5 minutes:

1. Stand up and stretch.
2. Look out the window.

10 minutes:

1. Take a quick walk.
2. Get a cup of coffee or bottle of water.
3. Use the restroom.

30-minute lunch:

1. Eat a light lunch (too much food or a meal that's too heavy will actually leave you more tired than you were before your lunch break).
2. Take a walk and get some fresh air.
3. Make a personal phone call.

60-minute lunch:

1. Eat a light lunch.
2. Take a walk to get some fresh air.
3. Run personal errands (this will give you a sense of accomplishment and allow you to have more personal time after work).

 *Assignment* *Task time: 10 minutes*

Schedule your breaks

Schedule your breaks on you BSG Daily Calendar by marking the time blocks. Get in the habit of taking your breaks at the same time allotted for them each day.

Chapter Nine: Find Balance

Be Smart Girls is dedicated to providing you with the tools you need to create balance in all facets of your life.

- Career

- Family

- Home

- Self

- Finances

If we did all the things we are capable of doing, we would literally astound ourselves.
—Thomas A. Edison

The "Smart" part of Be Smart Girls is to know how to use your time to your best advantage.

Do necessary but mundane chores like filing or housekeeping bog you down and sidetrack you from achieving your dreams? You may want to hire a housekeeper, personal trainer, life or business coach, or professional organizer. Consider hiring a part-time assistant for tasks that you know you do not have time for. The trade-off of "X" dollars for "X" hours of "me time" is well worth the investment.

Consider the following:

You make $_____ per hour.

You would be willing to pay $_____ per hour for just one extra hour per day of "me time." Your time is valuable so make your time ... time well spent. If you can budget this expense, go for it.

Lindsey's motto is "It is the start that stops you, so start today!"

- Focus on one small project that you can complete within 1 hour, and commit to doing it today.

- Progress breeds inspiration and long-term results.

- Use the Be Smart Girls Forms to schedule your day and track your time.

This publication focuses on your work environment and career. Visit www.BeSmartGirls.com to purchase additional Be Smart Girls guides to enhance your life or the lives of people you care about.

Be Smart Girls™

Guidelines for What to Keep and What to Throw Away
Task Sheet
Daily Calendar
Daily Priority Chart
List of Goals
Short-Term Goal Worksheet
Moderate-Term Goal Worksheet
Long-Term Goal Worksheet

For printable documents, please visit our Web site at
www.BeSmartGirls.com.

Be Smart Girls Guidelines for what to keep and what to throw away

Be extremely critical during this process. Consider the following as you evaluate each piece of paper:

- **Can you get this information somewhere else?** If you printed the information from a Web site, can you find it again using a quick search, adding to your favorites, and/or by saving it electronically? If yes, put in the recycle bin.

- **What is the worst-case scenario if you lost this paper?** Would you be released from your job? Lose a client? Go to prison? If you find the consequence isn't all that serious, then don't keep the paper. Put it in the recycle bin.

- **Keep all action items.** These are items that you must act on.

- **Keep all reference items.** We are referring to one-of-a-kind pieces of paper, something you can't get anywhere else. While doing this, ask yourself: Can I obtain this information from another department in the company? Or another resource? If yes, put it in the recycle bin.

- **Keep historical documents.** If you are going to keep these items, do not keep them in your office filing cabinet. At Be Smart Girls we consider this "prime real estate" and reserve it for active files only. You should archive historical documents. Refer to company, accounting, or industry-specific guidelines to determine what must be kept. As you go through this process, ask yourself, "Am I being a Smart Girl? Do I really need this paper?"

- **Limit magazines and catalogs.** Recycle all outdated catalogs and magazines. Be Smart Girls recommends setting a reading time to go through your magazines each week before the next issue arrives. If you are a department head and the information is a must-read, delegate reading assignments to other team or staff members. Have them report the highlights of the articles during weekly meetings. This allows for information sharing and decreases the amount of time dedicated to the interoffice transfer of reading materials.

Be Smart Girls Task Sheet	
Task	Time to Complete
Total Time Spent per Day	

Be Smart Girls Daily Calendar Today's Date: _____	
7:	
8:	
9:	
10:	
11:	
12:	
1:	
2:	
3:	
4:	
5:	

Be Smart Girls Daily Priority Chart
Date: _____

Priority 1 Tasks MUST DO Today (accomplish during most productive time of day)	Complete (x)
Priority 2 Tasks SHOULD DO Today (not until Priority 1 Tasks have been completed)	Complete (x)

Priority 3 Tasks WOULD LIKE TO DO Today (not at the expense of Priority 1 or 2 Tasks)	Complete (x)

List of Goals

In fifteen minutes, write ten to twenty things you want to do, have, or be. Remember: your goals can be as lofty or simple as you wish. Just write whatever comes to your mind. You can always edit them. Next to each goal create a timeline, a period in which you would like to accomplish these goals.

Short: 1 to 4 weeks; **Moderate:** 1 to 6 months; **Long:** 6 months or longer

Goal	Time

Short-Term Goal Worksheet

Respond to the following:

Choose a short-term goal from your list: _____

List 3 reasons for not accomplishing this goal yet:

-
-
-

Write why you feel you need to complete the goal or what the benefit is of completing this task:

-
-
-

What steps will you take to complete this goal?

-
-
-

Schedule time to complete the necessary steps in your BSG Daily Calendar and BSG Priority Chart.

Moderate-Term Goal Worksheet

Respond to the following:

Choose a moderate-term goal from your list: _____

List 3 reasons for not accomplishing this goal yet:

-
-
-

Write why you feel you need to complete the goal or what the benefit is of completing this task:

-
-
-

What steps will you take to complete this goal?

-
-
-

 Schedule time to complete the necessary steps in your BSG Daily Calendar and BSG Priority Chart.

Long-Term Goal Worksheet

Respond to the following:

Choose a long-term goal from your list: _____

List 3 reasons for not accomplishing this goal yet:

-
-
-

Write why you feel you need to complete the goal or what the benefit is of completing this task:

-
-
-

What steps will you take to complete this goal?

-
-
-

Schedule time to complete the necessary steps in your BSG Daily Calendar and BSG Priority Chart.

Congratulations on joining the Be Smart Girls team

Visit our website for more Be Smart Girls bright ideas and to sign up for your FREE Tip~A~Day 30 Days to a More Organized Life Calendar

www.BeSmartGirls.com

Watch for new products and guides to be launched soon!

Please contact our office at 619-861-9416 to schedule your FREE 15-minute consultation.

Need a speaker?

Dhawn and Tracey would love to speak at your upcoming event.

We offer company training seminars and Lunch-N-Learns that will teach your staff the techniques of time management and organization.

Topics:
- Time Management: Busy vs. Productive
- Project Management: Prioritize & Execute
- Business Success: Growth & Profitability
- Goal Setting: Believing & Achieving

Please contact our office at 619-861-9416 to schedule your FREE 15-minute consultation.

Need the personal touch?

Sign up for our one-on-one coaching programs.

Do you...

- Often start a project but don't finish it?
- Get overwhelmed in the middle of a project that you feel needs to be completed and then feel guilty because it is still staring at you a year later?
- Often come so close to completing a project but just can't find the stamina to finish it?

If so, we have programs to help you at all stages of goal achieving. Our programs are designed to help you fulfill your dreams. We have been told our programs live up to their names (Be Inspired, Be Motivated, and Be Empowered). Sign up for one of them and find out for yourself.

Please contact our office at 619-861-9416 to schedule your FREE 15-minute consultation.

About the Authors

Dhawn Hansen and Tracey Turner are the founders of Hansen Turner Solutions, LLC and the Be Smart Girls™ brand. As Certified Professional Organizers (CPO®) and time management experts, they provide consulting services to companies and individuals interested in achieving greater success while still having time for what matters most in life; family, friends and self. Hansen and Turner's passion for improving the lives of others has led them to create The Multi-Faceted Woman Seminar, teach Lunch-N-Learn programs, head discussion panels, and donate their time to St. Vincent de Paul, YMCA and other worthy charities. As recognized leaders, Dhawn is the Vice President of the National Association of Professional Organizers, San Diego chapter, and Tracey is the chapter Vice President of Business Network International. Their tips and techniques have been featured on NBC and in local and national publications.

Dhawn resides in San Diego, California, with her husband, Jeff. They are avid travelers, enjoying scuba diving the Great Barrier Reef, and hiking glaciers in Norway. Tracey also resides in San Diego, California, with her husband, David. They prefer exploring sights on land, their favorites being Japan, Indonesia, and Thailand.

978-0-595-42488-7
0-595-42488-0

Printed in the United States
92034LV00001B/1-99/A